Goodbye Little Dude

Written by Rebecca Trotsky with Marie Smyth

Illustrated by Steve Dansereau

ISBN 978-1-970002-00-3 (hardcover) and 978-1-970002-01-0 (softcover)

www.goodbyelittledude.com

For Jonathan

It was early fall. Jonathan and his mom were in the car returning home from a doctor's appointment.

"Some days are longer than others," Jonathan thought to himself. "I wish I could skip these doctors' appointments and just play soccer outside with my friends. I hope I feel better soon."

"Jonathan, are you hungry?" his mom asked as they drove along.

"A little," he replied. As his mom pulled into his favorite donut shop, Jonathan's stomach growled from the medicine. A donut would taste great right now, he thought. This was their usual stop on the way home.

He climbed out of the car and noticed the sweet, familiar smell of baked goods. This place had so many good things to eat that it was always hard to choose just one treat.

"May I please have a chocolate-glazed donut?" Jonathan asked as he peered over the counter at the fresh-baked goodies.

"You certainly may," said the woman behind the counter.

Now that he could read, Jonathan noticed her nametag said "Ann" on it. She seemed very nice.

"I like your hat," Ann said as she handed him a brown bag with his donut inside.

"Thank you," Jonathan replied. "I always wear it because my hair is a little thin from all the medicine I take. Plus, I'm a huge Red Sox fan!"

"You're lucky that you look fantastic in hats. Not everyone looks so good in hats, you know. Just look at me!" She smiled at him from under the brim of her own hat as he thanked her for the donut and left the store.

"She's right," Jonathan thought. "I do look pretty cool in hats." His mom squeezed his hand and gave him a big smile as they walked to the car.

When Jonathan reached the car, he looked down into his bag to get his donut. As he did, he noticed something moving on the ground below him. When he looked again, he saw a very small, very scared little turtle.

"Mom!" he yelled as he dropped the bag, completely forgetting about the delicious treat it held inside. "Look what I found! This poor little turtle is all alone and looks very scared. He must have crawled out of the stream over there. He's lost, and maybe even lonely. Can we please keep him? I will care for him and make him feel better."

"Jonathan," said his mom, "don't you think we should leave him here so maybe he'll find his family?"

"No, Mom," Jonathan replied. "Trust me. I know he needs me. We can't leave him. He can come to school with me for show and tell. My whole class can help care for him and become his family."

Jonathan's eyes said it all. His mom knew he would be a great parent to his new little friend. She knew his heart was big enough to love the turtle and to see he got everything he needed to grow big and strong.

"Okay, Jonathan." His mom emptied her coffee cup and gave it to Jonathan with a napkin. "Put him in my coffee cup until we get home. Be sure not to touch him."

"Thanks, Mom!" Jonathan exclaimed as he closed his car door. "I promise to let him go in our pond when he's big and healthy and strong enough to play with his own friends."

Jonathan and the turtle settled into the car. "Little Dude," Jonathan said.

"What?" asked his mom.

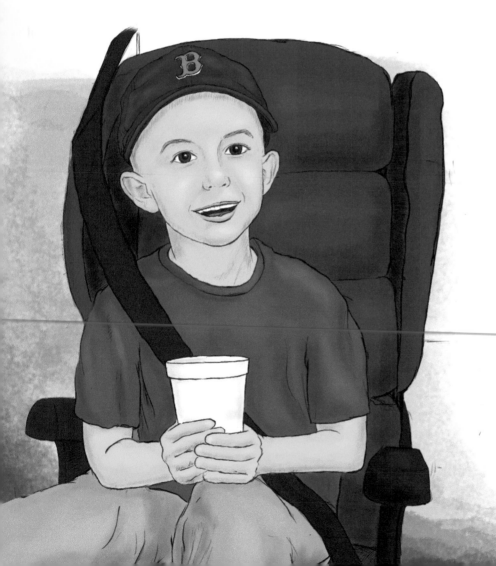

"Little Dude for his name!" he exclaimed.

"Jonathan," his mom replied, "he's your turtle. If you want to name him Little Dude, you should. I think it's a terrific name."

As they pulled away from the donut shop, Jonathan knew he would do a great job caring for his new friend.

At home, Jonathan found an old, empty fish bowl and got to work. He added dirt, weeds, a little water, plenty of twigs, and a rock. It was a special rock so Little Dude could climb out of the water to warm himself in the sun. It would be a perfect home for Little Dude, and Little Dude was the perfect friend to keep Jonathan busy while he was at home.

When Jonathan was ready to return to school, Little Dude was ready to go with him. Ms. Carney's first-grade class would never be the same again. Little Dude (and his bowl) moved right in and took his place on the windowsill.

Jonathan assigned jobs to care for Little Dude to his classmates. He knew there would be days when he would not be in school, so he wanted to make sure Little Dude always had everything he needed.

Jonathan's classmates took their jobs of caring for Little Dude very seriously. They wanted him to grow up big and strong and live a healthy turtle life. They were proud to be responsible for a small creature and they were happy to help Jonathan in any way they could.

They fed him once a day. He loved his special turtle food. They cleaned his fish bowl once a week. They made sure their parents and teachers helped to get everything they needed for Little Dude.

Little Dude became a member of the class. He said the Pledge of Allegiance every morning with his friends. He watched them play dodge ball in gym class. He went to music and art classes.

The children learned all about turtles and how to care for them. Little Dude was their very own living science project! He thrived under their care.

Ms. Carney read many books to the children about turtles. They often took books home from the library to learn as much as they could about their class pet.

Whenever Jonathan was too sick to come to school, Little Dude would remind everyone to send Jonathan get-well cards and letters. They missed their friend Jonathan and wished he would come back to school soon.

As winter came, Little Dude was so healthy that he grew too big for his bowl. Jonathan and his dad built him a new home in a bigger aquarium. It had tape on one side where there was a crack in the glass. The crack didn't bother Little Dude.

In the early spring, there were a few days when Jonathan was strong enough to go to school. He could even play outside at recess with his twenty-two classmates and Little Dude. On those days, the other children were given special permission to wear their favorite baseball hat, too, just like their good friend Jonathan. But those days didn't last.

As Little Dude grew bigger and stronger, Jonathan grew weaker. It was becoming more difficult for him to go to school. The students in Ms. Carney's first-grade class were worried about Jonathan and wanted to help him. They couldn't make Jonathan better, but they could be sure that Little Dude was happy and healthy.

By June, the school year was coming to an end. Soon it would be summer and the class would scatter for summer vacations. Jonathan's classmates could see that Little Dude was getting too big for his tank. They knew he was ready to meet new turtle friends. He had grown so big and strong that Little Dude had become Big Dude!

Just before the school year ended, Little Dude went home with Jonathan. Jonathan knew his classmates were right. It would soon be time to say goodbye to his turtle friend.

Jonathan was happy for Little Dude because he had grown up healthy and strong and was ready to meet new turtle friends. At the same time, he felt very sad that he would have to say goodbye to someone so special to him. It sure was confusing.

On the last day of school,
Jonathan invited Ms. Carney,
the whole class, and all their
moms and dads to a big
going-away celebration for
Little Dude. You see, Jonathan
had a pond in his backyard
that would be Little Dude's
new home. This party would
be the last time the whole
class would ever be together.

After eating popsicles, playing
games, and celebrating the
fun year they had together, it
was time for everyone to head
out to the pond. Ms. Carney
carried Little Dude, Jonathan
was carried by his mom, and
the whole class followed
behind in a line down the
path to the pond.

This was it! When they reached the pond, Ms. Carney bent down and put Little Dude in the water. Little Dude looked up out of his shell at Jonathan and his classmates as if to say, "Goodbye and thank you." Then, with one big dive, he was gone. Little Dude was free and on his way to make new turtle friends.

Everyone waved goodbye as he swam away.

Just then, Jonathan was feeling a new kind of pain. Unlike when he gets his medicine and his body hurts, this pain hurt in his heart. He realized how hard it was to say goodbye to someone you love, even when you know they'll be in a better place. He looked around at the faces on his friends and knew they were feeling the same way.

As the day ended, Jonathan's classmates thanked him for the party, and especially for sharing Little Dude with them all year. These friends would never forget their remarkable first-grade year. While caring for their friends, Jonathan and Little Dude, they learned that sometimes you have to say goodbye to someone you love.

As the years passed, Jonathan's mom would occasionally see a happy and healthy Little Dude living in the pond. Seeing Little Dude would comfort her and remind her of the smile on Jonathan's face the day he said goodbye.

Goodbye Little Dude.

Jonathan's Story . . .

The day Little Dude was released into Jonathan's pond left an indelible mark on Jonathan's classmates. Becky, a classmate's mother, was so moved by the experience that she went home and wrote *Goodbye Little Dude*.

Six months later, Jonathan succumbed to cancer in January 1998. He suffered from neuroblastoma. To this day, it is still the third most common form of childhood cancer. School for him had been a pleasant diversion in between cancer treatments at the Dana-Farber Cancer Institute in Boston.

From the moment Jonathan's treatment began, his mother, Marie, became involved with fundraising efforts at Dana-Farber. While Jonathan was still alive, his family and classmates participated in the Boston Marathon Jimmy Fund Walk. Marie pushed Jonathan in a wheelchair decorated with pictures drawn by his classmates while they surrounded him on foot. They continued to walk together as a team year after year, long after their beloved Jonathan had passed away.

Jonathan's classmates are adults now, but they will never forget their first-grade year. Jonathan and his sweet turtle, Little Dude, both made a lasting impression on their young lives.

Becky gifted the *Goodbye Little Dude* manuscript to Marie following Jonathan's funeral. It sat in Marie's desk drawer for over 17 years before she could open her heart to look at it.

After all those years, Becky answered the phone the first time Marie called. Not close friends when their sons were in first grade together, they are now like family. That first two-hour conversation has led them to the publication of this beautiful story.

Marie's dedication to the hospital that treated her young son has never wavered. She has continued to be very involved in fundraising efforts for Dana-Farber. Profits from the sale of this book will be donated directly to Dana-Farber for continued research in the fight against childhood cancer.

Fate also brought Amy Shields Mack into Marie's life. Jonathan and Amy's mother, Patricia Shields, both battled cancer and received treatment at Dana-Farber. Residents of Sudbury, Massachusetts, Jonathan and Patricia are buried only two gravestones apart. Amy often noticed the Lego-shaped gravestone so close to her mother's and wondered about the seven-year-old boy who died too young.

In 2008, Amy joined the Dana-Farber Marathon Challenge team to run the Boston Marathon to honor her mom. Amy's dad recognized Jonathan Smyth's name at a marathon event. The next year, Amy decided to run the marathon in Jonathan's memory. With great excitement, Amy shared with Marie their connection—that special place at the far corner of Wadsworth Cemetery. An immediate bond of kinship was forged.

Marie shared with Amy her dream to have *Goodbye Little Dude* illustrated and published in Jonathan's memory. In 2014, Amy connected Marie with her good friend and illustrator Steve Dansereau. Amy's sister, Regan, introduced Marie to her friend and publisher Damaris Curran Herlihy. What you hold in your hands is their final labor of love.

This true story about Jonathan and his beloved turtle Little Dude was written to honor Jonathan's life and his memory. We hope it will provide comfort to other families dealing with the loss of a loved one. By donating the proceeds of this book to pediatric cancer research, we hope to make a difference in the fight against childhood cancer. This picture book was only made possible by the tremendous amount of help and support we received from our family and friends. Out of unbearable pain and loss grew a new, unique, and wonderful family. By telling his story, we honor Jonathan's memory and so many other angels in heaven.

—The *Goodbye Little Dude* Family

CPSIA information can be obtained
at www.ICGtesting.com
Printed in the USA
LVHW07n0320050418
572383LV00021B/318/P